Easy Peasy
TIMES
TABLES

What are numbers?

Numbers are what we use to count things.
We can count all sorts of things...

Animals

People

Places

Objects

Units of measurement

Numbers can either be written as words or as symbols called numerals.

two   six

five   eight

5   8

6   2

Counting

Let's start by counting the objects below.

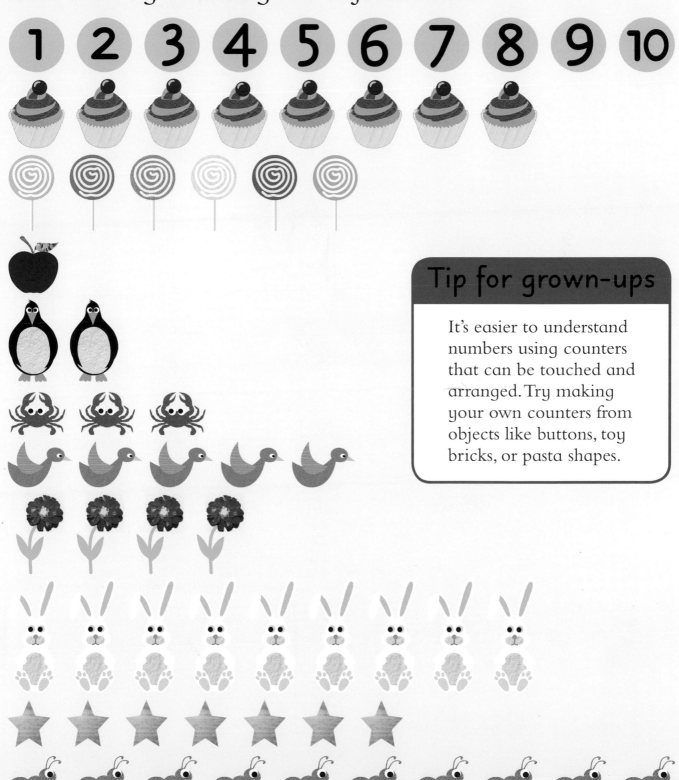

Tip for grown-ups

It's easier to understand numbers using counters that can be touched and arranged. Try making your own counters from objects like buttons, toy bricks, or pasta shapes.

5

Multiplication

It's easy to count small numbers of things.
But what if you have lots of things to count?

If we have lots of things to count,
it can be easier to count in groups.

We can count the socks in pairs.
There are 2 socks in every pair.

A jumble of socks.

2 + 2 + 2 + 2 + 2 = 10 socks

This sum uses ADDITION.

How many pairs do we have? We have 5 pairs of socks.
This sum can also be written as

5 × 2 = 10 socks

This time we're using
MULTIPLICATION.

5 × 2 is the same as **2 × 5**.
The sums are written in different
ways but their answers are the same.

Another way of saying "multiplied by" is to say "TIMES".
The multiplication, or times, sign is **×**.

How many groups of apples do we have in these fruit bowls?

3 lots of 3 apples.

$3 \times 3 = 9$ apples in total.

How many fish are in these fish bowls?

2 lots of 4 fish.

Multiplication is a quick way of adding up the same number over and over again.

$2 \times 4 = 8$ fish in total.

Can you match up these addition and multiplication sums?

4 × 7

3 + 3 + 3

7 × 4

4 + 4 + 4 + 4 + 4 + 4 + 4

7 + 7 + 7 + 7

3 × 3

Tip for grown-ups

Adding and multiplying will be easier to understand if you start by drawing the number groupings or using homemade counters.

Times tables

Multiplication is quick and easy if we know our times tables. Times tables aren't pieces of furniture. They are mathematical tables that show us multiplication sums and answers.

The 1 times table is super easy.

1×

$1 \times 1 = 1$

$2 \times 1 = 2$

$3 \times 1 = 3$

$4 \times 1 = 4$

$5 \times 1 = 5$

$6 \times 1 = 6$

$7 \times 1 = 7$

$8 \times 1 = 8$

$9 \times 1 = 9$

$10 \times 1 = 10$

$11 \times 1 = 11$

$12 \times 1 = 12$

"1 times" means having 1 group of something.

1 bowl with 3 apples.
How many apples? **3**

1 bag of 7 sweets.
How many sweets? **7**

1 dog with 4 feet.
How many feet? **4**

Number patterns

The other times tables will be easier to remember if you get to know their number patterns.
What number patterns can you see here?

Look at each number square and get to know the pattern for each times table.

These numbers are **odd** numbers.

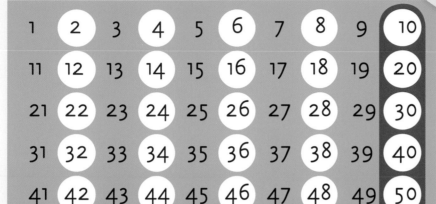

These numbers all end in 0. They are all found in the 10 times table.

The numbers in white are **even** numbers. This is the pattern of the 2 times table.

Odd and even numbers

Numbers are either **odd numbers** or **even numbers**.

Odd numbers end in 1, 3, 5, 7, 9.
Even numbers end in 2, 4, 6, 8, 0.

1 2 3 4 5 6 7 8 9 10

Tip for grown-ups

This is a great time for colouring-in. Copy the number square out together and spend time colouring in the number pattern for each times table.

At the zoo with the twos

Lots of things come in twos – socks, shoes, hands, feet, eyes, and ears. Can you think of anything else?

How many penguins are there in this icy enclosure?
They're standing in pairs so let's count them in 2s:

2   4   6   8   10

It's feeding time at the zoo.
The zookeeper must feed the
animals in the even-numbered pens.
Which animals are these?

I'm hungry!

How many pairs of flamingos are there?

Tip for grown-ups

Find opportunities to say the 2 times table together. Give it a try while pairing up socks, walking up the stairs, or passing houses in the street.

All the answers in the 2 × table are called "multiples" of 2.

$1 \times 2 = 2$

$2 \times 2 = 4$

$3 \times 2 = 6$

$4 \times 2 = 8$

$5 \times 2 = 10$

$6 \times 2 = 12$

$7 \times 2 = 14$

$8 \times 2 = 16$

$9 \times 2 = 18$

$10 \times 2 = 20$

$11 \times 2 = 22$

$12 \times 2 = 24$

$2 \times 6 = \underline{}$

How many legs do 6 flamingos have?

There are 3 pairs of flamingos.

Getting tiny with the tens

How many spots do the ladybirds have?

$3 \times 10 = 30$

The 10 times table is easy to learn. To multiply any whole number by 10, just add a 0 on the end.

2 3 4 5 6 7 8 9 10 1

Remember to add the 0.

$1 \times 10 = 1\,0$
$2 \times 10 = 2\,0$
$3 \times 10 = 3\,\_$
$4 \times 10 = \_\_\_$

Look, here are 10 ants walking in a row.

How many ants are there now?

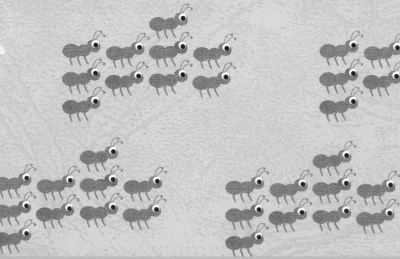

$4 \times 10 = 40$

How many flies are zipping around?

Making numbers BIGGER

Let's make these numbers 10 times bigger! Remember, we do this by adding 0 to the end of each number.

×10

4⁰ 7⁰ 3⁰

9 2

40 90 70 20 30

1 × 10 = 10

2 × 10 = 20

3 × 10 = 30

4 × 10 = 40

5 × 10 = 50

6 × 10 = 60

7 × 10 = 70

8 × 10 = 80

9 × 10 = 90

10 × 10 = 100

11 × 10 = 110

12 × 10 = 120

How many seeds are there?

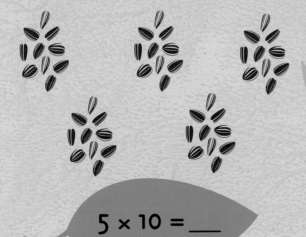

5 × 10 = ___

In the sky with the fives

When you count in 5s, every other number ends in 5. All of the numbers in between end in a 0.

5 10 15 20 25 30 35 40 45 50...

There are 5 birds flying in this flock.

How many birds are flying in 4 flocks?

$4 \times 5 = 20$

Numbers in the 5 times table end with either a 5 or a 0.

How many birds are there in 5 flocks of 5?

The multiples of 5 run in two lines down the number square.

1	2	3	4	5	6	7	8	9	10
11	12	13	14	15	16	17	18	19	20
21	22	23	24	25	26	27	28	29	30
31	32	33	34	35	36	37	38	39	40
41	42	43	44	45	46	47	48	49	50
51	52	53	54	55	56	57	58	59	60
61	62	63	64	65	66	67	68	69	70
71	72	73	74	75	76	77	78	79	80
81	82	83	84	85	86	87	88	89	90
91	92	93	94	95	96	97	98	99	100

5×

$1 \times 5 = 5$

$2 \times 5 = 10$

$3 \times 5 = 15$

$4 \times 5 = 20$

$5 \times 5 = 25$

$6 \times 5 = 30$

$7 \times 5 = 35$

$8 \times 5 = 40$

$9 \times 5 = 45$

$10 \times 5 = 50$

$11 \times 5 = 55$

$12 \times 5 = 60$

Some bunches of balloons have drifted up into the sky. There are 5 balloons in each bunch.

Tip for grown-ups

You can use the five-day school week to work through the 5 times table together. How many school days are there in two weeks? Keep going until you get to 12 weeks.

There are _____ bunches of balloons.
There are _____ balloons in total.

25 birds.

Under the sea with the threes

How many birds are there?

$2 \times 3 = 6$

With a little help from under the sea, learning your 3 times table will be as easy as 1, 2, 3.

1 **3**
2

These fish are swimming together in a group of 3.

Tip for grown-ups

Repeating the times tables out loud helps children to remember them. Making the 3 times table into a song or a sea shanty will make it even more memorable!

How many fish are there in 2 groups of 3?

How many crabs are scuttling along the sand?

$3 \times 3 = 9$

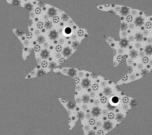

$2 \times 3 = 6$

16   How many fish are swimming in the sea?

3×

1 × 3 = 3

2 × 3 = 6

3 × 3 = 9

4 × 3 = 12

5 × 3 = 15

6 × 3 = 18

7 × 3 = 21

8 × 3 = 24

9 × 3 = 27

10 × 3 = 30

11 × 3 = 33

12 × 3 = 36

Because 3 is an odd number, its multiples are alternately odd and even numbers.

How many coins are piled up on the sand?

5 × 3 = ___

In the garden with the fours

Let's try counting in 4s. Remember, 4 is an even number and all of its multiples will be even numbers too.

4   8   12   16   20   24...

1   2   3   4

Here are 4 plants. Each plant has one yellow flower. How many flowers are there? 4 of course!

How many red flowers are in the garden?

2 × 4 = 8

How many snails are there in the garden?

Multiples of 4 end with the numbers **0, 2, 4, 6,** or **8.** Look, this pattern is repeated all through the square!

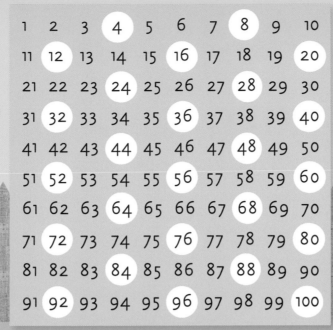

1	2	3	4	5	6	7	8	9	10
11	12	13	14	15	16	17	18	19	20
21	22	23	24	25	26	27	28	29	30
31	32	33	34	35	36	37	38	39	40
41	42	43	44	45	46	47	48	49	50
51	52	53	54	55	56	57	58	59	60
61	62	63	64	65	66	67	68	69	70
71	72	73	74	75	76	77	78	79	80
81	82	83	84	85	86	87	88	89	90
91	92	93	94	95	96	97	98	99	100

4×

$$1 \times 4 = 4$$

$$2 \times 4 = 8$$

$$3 \times 4 = 12$$

$$4 \times 4 = 16$$

$$5 \times 4 = 20$$

$$6 \times 4 = 24$$

$$7 \times 4 = 28$$

$$8 \times 4 = 32$$

$$9 \times 4 = 36$$

$$10 \times 4 = 40$$

$$11 \times 4 = 44$$

$$12 \times 4 = 48$$

If the rabbit takes a nibble out of every 4th carrot in the row, which carrots will he eat?

1   2   3   4   5   6   7   8   9   10   11   12

Tip for grown-ups

The morning is the best time to test and practise times tables – when brains are fresh and children are energized. Short bursts of activity are more effective than long sessions.

Magic time with the nines

The 9 times table may seem a little difficult but the wise old owl can show you a trick or two.

That's magic! The owl has produced 9 white rabbits from his top hat.

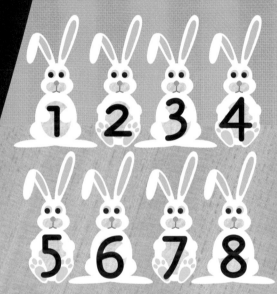

How many rabbits has the hat produced this time?

$2 \times 9 = 18$

How many rabbits in total?

As you go through the 9 times table, the first digit in the number goes up by 1 and the last digit goes down by 1 each time.

1	2	3	4	5	6	7	8	9	10
11	12	13	14	15	16	17	18	19	20
21	22	23	24	25	26	27	28	29	30
31	32	33	34	35	36	37	38	39	40
41	42	43	44	45	46	47	48	49	50
51	52	53	54	55	56	57	58	59	60
61	62	63	64	65	66	67	68	69	70
71	72	73	74	75	76	77	78	79	80
81	82	83	84	85	86	87	88	89	90
91	92	93	94	95	96	97	98	99	100

9 ×

$1 × 9 = 9$

$2 × 9 = 18$

$3 × 9 = 27$

$4 × 9 = 36$

$5 × 9 = 45$

$6 × 9 = 54$

$7 × 9 = 63$

$8 × 9 = 72$

$9 × 9 = 81$

$10 × 9 = 90$

$11 × 9 = 99$

$12 × 9 = 108$

The magic number

The number 9 and its multiples are special numbers. Each multiple of 9 can be broken down and added together to produce… the number 9!

$2 × 9 = 1\ 8$

$1 + 8 = 9$

$3 × 9 = 2\ 7$

$2 + 7 = 9$

Which of these numbers are multiples of 9?

32   56   27   93   54   9

15   73   44   81   72

At the sweet shop with the sixes

Life is sweeter when you know your times tables, and it's easier to work out prices and amounts in shops.

1 2 3 4 5 6

Here are 6 large lollipops, all bright and sugary.

Here are 2 groups of 6 lollipops.
How many are there now?

$2 \times 6 = 12$

Remember, you can write the sum 2×6 or 6×2, the answer will be the same.

How many marshmallows are in these bags?

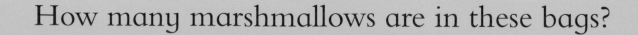

1	2	3	4	5	6	7	8	9	10
11	12	13	14	15	16	17	18	19	20
21	22	23	24	25	26	27	28	29	30
31	32	33	34	35	36	37	38	39	40
41	42	43	44	45	46	47	48	49	50
51	52	53	54	55	56	57	58	59	60
61	62	63	64	65	66	67	68	69	70
71	72	73	74	75	76	77	78	79	80
81	82	83	84	85	86	87	88	89	90
91	92	93	94	95	96	97	98	99	100

6×

The multiples of 6 form rows running diagonally across the number square.

$1 \times 6 = 6$

$2 \times 6 = 12$

$3 \times 6 = 18$

$4 \times 6 = 24$

$5 \times 6 = 30$

$6 \times 6 = 36$

$7 \times 6 = 42$

$8 \times 6 = 48$

$9 \times 6 = 54$

$10 \times 6 = 60$

$11 \times 6 = 66$

$12 \times 6 = 72$

Each jar on this shelf contains 6 sweets. How many sweets are there in total?

$5 \times 6 = \underline{\quad}$

Tip for grown-ups

Time to raid the piggy bank! Practise multiplying with real money or when you're in a shop. This will show how useful the times tables can be.

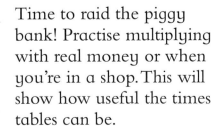

There are 24 marshmallows.

In the heavens with the sevens

We're reaching the heights with our times tables now. Once you've learned your 7 times table, you'll be one step nearer to becoming a master of multiplication.

⭐ 1 ⭐ 3 ⭐ 5 ⭐ 7
⭐ 2 ⭐ 4 ⭐ 6

Here is a cluster of 7 stars.

How many stars are there in 3 clusters of 7?

$3 \times 7 = 21$

How many shooting stars can you see?

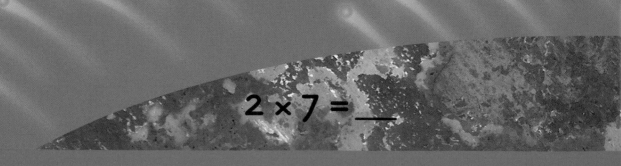

$2 \times 7 = \underline{}$

How many antennae do the Martians have?

1	2	3	4	5	6	**7**	8	9	10
11	12	13	**14**	15	16	17	18	19	20
21	22	23	24	25	26	27	**28**	29	30
31	32	33	34	**35**	36	37	38	39	40
41	**42**	43	44	45	46	47	48	**49**	50
51	52	53	54	55	**56**	57	58	59	60
61	62	**63**	64	65	66	67	68	69	**70**
71	72	73	74	75	76	**77**	78	79	80
81	82	83	**84**	85	86	87	88	89	90
91	92	93	94	95	96	97	**98**	99	100

7×

$1 \times 7 = 7$

$2 \times 7 = 14$

$3 \times 7 = 21$

$4 \times 7 = 28$

$5 \times 7 = 35$

$6 \times 7 = 42$

$7 \times 7 = 49$

$8 \times 7 = 56$

$9 \times 7 = 63$

$10 \times 7 = 70$

$11 \times 7 = 77$

$12 \times 7 = 84$

Multiplying Martians

These creatures are Martians. They live in outer space. Each Martian has:

3 antennae

4 eyes

5 arms

8 legs

How many eyes, legs, and arms do we have in total?

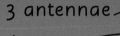

$7 \times 4 = \underline{}$ eyes
$7 \times 8 = \underline{}$ legs
$7 \times 5 = \underline{}$ arms

They have 21 antennae in total.

25

Baking cakes with the eights

The multiples of 8 are all even numbers.

The times tables come in really useful when we're baking and making things. They can help us to work out the right amounts.

Here are 8 little cakes, covered in pink icing. They look yummy!

If we make twice as many cakes, how many will we have?

$$2 \times 8 = 16$$

"Twice as many" means the same as 2 times the number of cakes.

Tip for grown-ups

Practice makes perfect. Lots of repetition will get the times tables stuck in children's heads. Try asking quick-fire questions to test their knowledge and give rewards for the correct answers.

How many cherries are there?

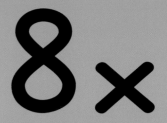

8 ×

1	2	3	4	5	6	7	**8**	9	10
11	12	13	14	15	**16**	17	18	19	20
21	22	23	**24**	25	26	27	28	29	30
31	**32**	33	34	35	36	37	38	39	**40**
41	42	43	44	45	46	47	**48**	49	50
51	52	53	54	55	**56**	57	58	59	60
61	62	63	**64**	65	66	67	68	69	70
71	**72**	73	74	75	76	77	78	79	**80**
81	82	83	84	85	86	87	**88**	89	90
91	92	93	94	95	**96**	97	98	99	100

$1 \times 8 = 8$

$2 \times 8 = 16$

$3 \times 8 = 24$

$4 \times 8 = 32$

$5 \times 8 = 40$

$6 \times 8 = 48$

$7 \times 8 = 56$

$8 \times 8 = 64$

$9 \times 8 = 72$

$10 \times 8 = 80$

$11 \times 8 = 88$

$12 \times 8 = 96$

Oh no! We've made quite a mess. Can you work out what the missing numbers are?

$8 \times 3 =$

$8 \times = 72$

$4 \times = 32$

$8 \times 12 =$

$7 \times 8 =$

$10 \times 8 =$

$ \times 8 = 16$

Activities

Here are some fun puzzles to test your times tables knowledge.

Take your time solving these puzzles and practise any times tables you find it hard to remember.

Spaghetti tangle

Can you untangle this puzzle and find the matching pairs?

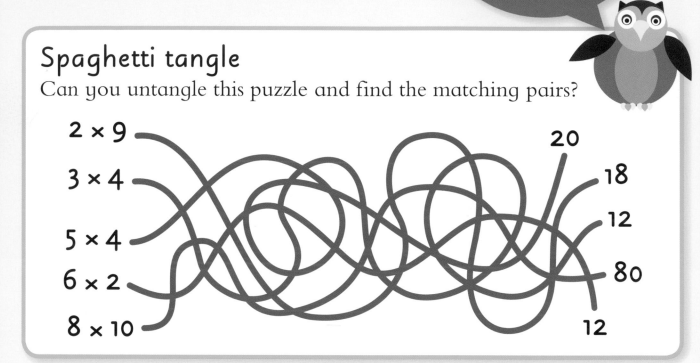

2 × 9
3 × 4
5 × 4
6 × 2
8 × 10

20
18
12
80
12

Give a dog a home

Can you work out which kennel belongs to each dog?

45   40   48   27   35

4 × 10   7 × 5   3 × 9   8 × 6   5 × 9

Going fishing

Match the number on each fish to the times table it appears in.

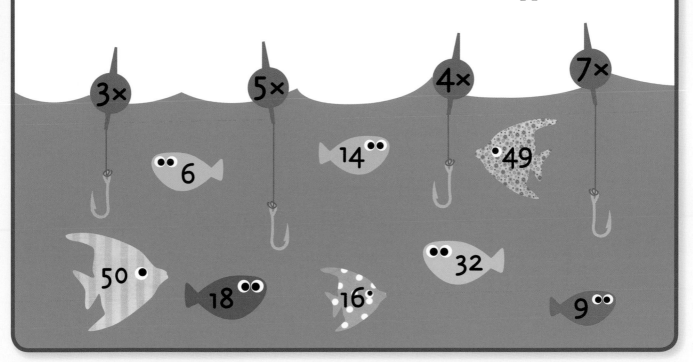

Missing numbers

Which person is needed to complete each multiplication?

$$2 \times \; ? \; = 18$$

$$? \times 4 = 28$$

$$5 \times 5 = \; ?$$

$$6 \times \; ? \; = 24$$

 9
 6
 20
 4
 7
 25

11×

1 × 11 = 11

2 × 11 = 22

3 × 11 = 33

4 × 11 = 44

5 × 11 = 55

6 × 11 = 66

7 × 11 = 77

8 × 11 = 88

9 × 11 = 99

10 × 11 = 110

11 × 11 = 121

12 × 11 = 132

Once you've mastered times tables 1 to 10, why not give these a try?

11 times table

The 11 times table is really easy up to 9 × 11, because the answer is the original number written twice.

1 × 11 = 11
2 × 11 = 22
3 × 11 = 33

Now you try!

12 times table

If you've been paying attention, you should already know nearly all of these multiplication answers from the other times tables.

This is the only new one

12×

1 × 12 = 12

2 × 12 = 24

3 × 12 = 36

4 × 12 = 48

5 × 12 = 60

6 × 12 = 72

7 × 12 = 84

8 × 12 = 96

9 × 12 = 108

10 × 12 = 120

11 × 12 = 132

12 × 12 = 144